To K

A very happy Christmas

With love from

Pat and Don

1997

Peer Gynt Suite, Holberg Suite
and Other Works for Piano Solo

EDVARD GRIEG

DOVER PUBLICATIONS, INC.
New York

Published in Canada by General Publishing Company, Ltd., 30 Lesmill Road, Don Mills, Toronto, Ontario.
Published in the United Kingdom by Constable and Company, Ltd., 3 The Lanchesters, 162–164 Fulham Palace Road, London W6 9ER.

This Dover edition, first published in 1993, is a republication of portions of Volumes II and III of *Werke für Klavier zu 2 Händen* and the complete *Sonate for Piano*, all originally published by C. F. Peters, Leipzig, n.d.

Manfactured in the United States of America
Dover Publications, Inc.
31 East 2nd Street
Mineola, NY 11501

Library of Congress Cataloging-in-Publication Data

Grieg, Edvard, 1843–1907.
  [Instrumental music.   Selections]
  Peer Gynt suite, Holberg suite, and other works for piano solo/Edvard Grieg.
    p. of music.
  "Republication of portions of volumes 2 and 3 of Werke für Klavier zu 2 Händen and the complete Sonate for piano, all originally published by C.F. Peters, Leipzig, n.d."—T.p. verso.
  Contents: Four pieces, op. 1—Poetic tone-pictures—Humoresques, op. 6—Sonata in E minor, op. 7—Concerto in A minor, op. 16, arr. for piano solo—Four album leaves—Two elegiac melodies—From Holberg's time—Piano pieces after his own songs : (I)—Peer Gynt suite : no. 1, op. 46—Piano pieces after his own songs : (II)—Two melodies, op. 53—Peer Gynt suite : no. 2, op. 55—Moods—Nordraak's funeral march—Three piano pieces, WoOp.
  ISBN 0-486-27590-6 (pbk.)
  1. Piano music.   2. Suites (Piano)   3. Piano music, Arranged.   I. Title.
M25.G   92-30691
                                                                                          CIP
                                                                                            M

CONTENTS

The dates are those of composition. The arrangements of orchestral works have the same opus numbers as the original versions.

Peer Gynt Suite, Holberg Suite
and Other Works for Piano Solo

Four Pieces, Op. 1
Vier Stücke
I.

Allegro con leggerezza

II.

Non Allegro e molto espressivo

III.
Mazurka

IV.

Poetic Tone-Pictures, Op. 3
Poetiske tonebilleder
I.

II.

III.

IV.

V.

VI.

Humoresques, Op. 6
Humoresker
I.

II.

Tempo di Menuetto ed energico

III.

Allegretto con grazia

IV.

Allegro alla burla

Sonata in E Minor, Op. 7

Alla Menuetto, ma poco più lento.

Finale.

Molto allegro.

Concerto in A Minor, Op. 16
Arranged for Solo Piano

*) The 32nd notes are to be executed like grace notes, *pp* and with extreme delicacy.

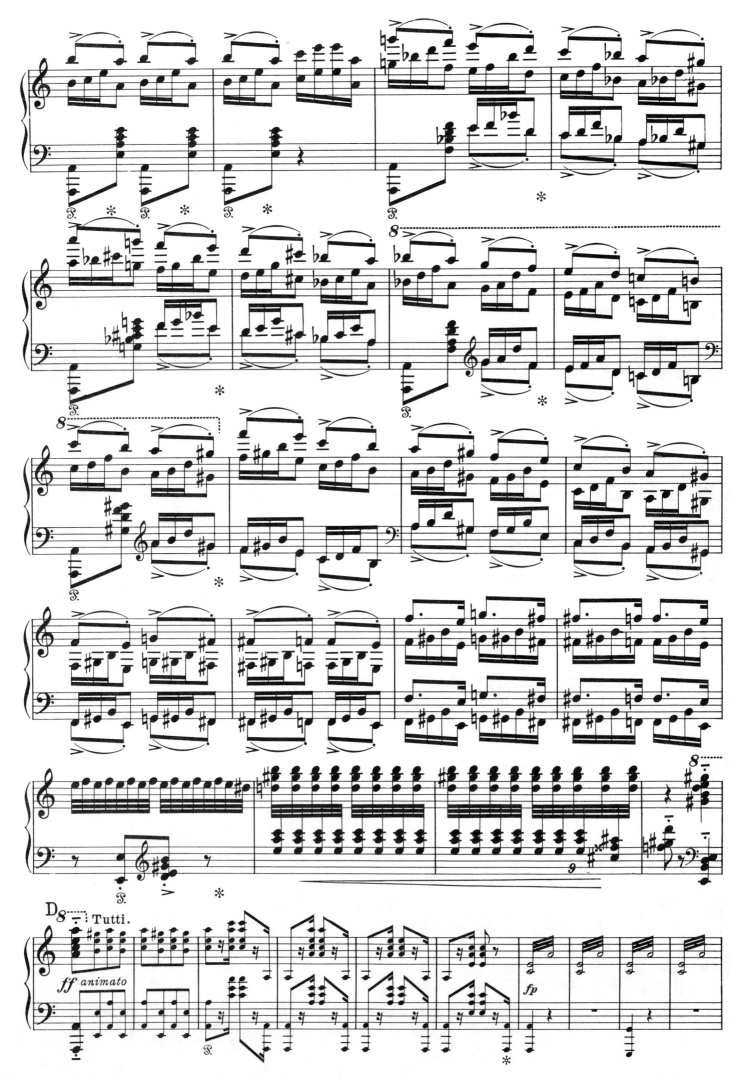

Tempo I animato.
Tutti.

Solo.

un poco marcato

Pedale sempre come la I^{ma} volta

cresc. e stringendo

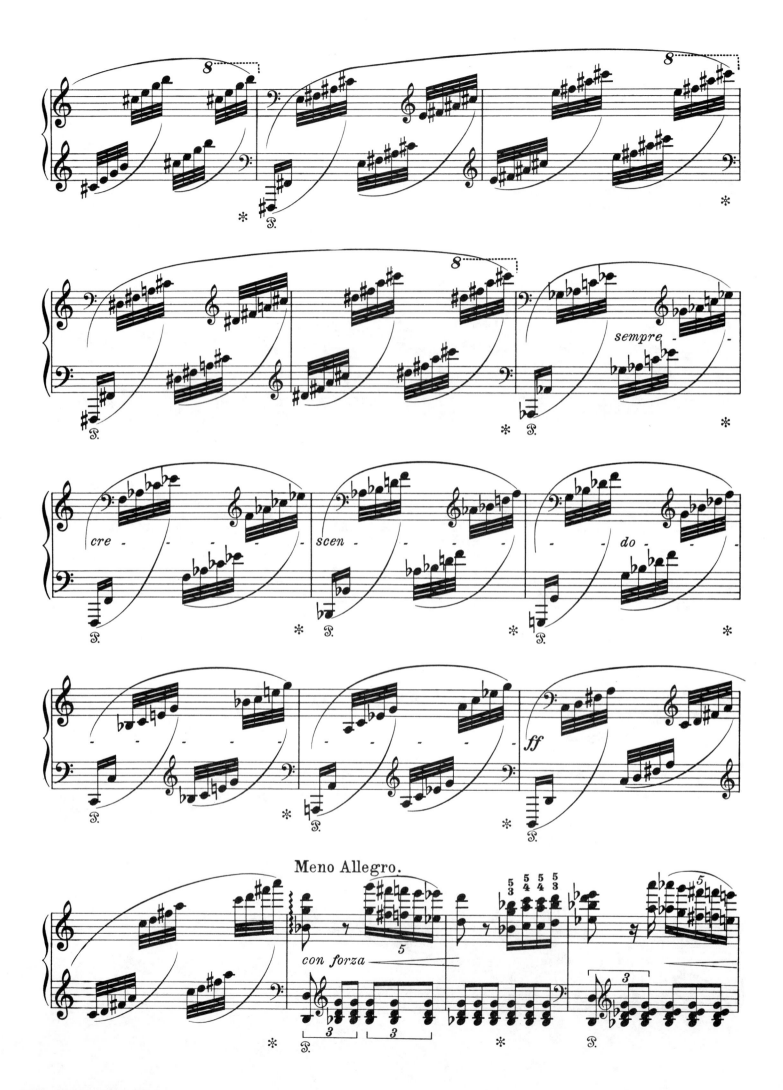

Four Album Leaves, Op. 28
Fire albumblade
I.

II.

III.

IV.

Two Elegiac Melodies, Op. 34
Zwei elegische Melodien
I.

Heart's Wounds
(Herzwunden; Den saerde)

II.
Last Spring
(Letzter Frühling; Våren)

From Holberg's Time [Holberg Suite], Op. 40
Fra Holbergs tid
I.
Praeludium

From Holberg's Time [Holberg Suite]

II.
Sarabande

Andante espressivo ♩ = 52

III.
Gavotte

MUSETTE

Un poco più mosso

Gavotte da Capo al Fine

IV.
Air

V.
Rigaudon

From Holberg's Time [Holberg Suite]

TRIO

Rigaudon da capo al fine,
ma senza repetizione.

From Holberg's Time [Holberg Suite] 135

Piano Pieces after His Own Songs (I), Op. 41
Klavierstücke nach eigenen Liedern
I.
Lullaby
(Wiegenlied; Vuggesang)

II.
Little Haakon
(Klein Haakon; Margretes vuggesang)

Andante e ben tenuto.

Nun schloß die Au-gen bei-de zum Schlaf klein Haa-kon kaum, da

sieht er schon mit La-chen den al-ler-schön-sten Traum. Es baut sich ei-ne

Stie-ge hin-auf zum Him-mels-zelt, drauf stei-gen Got-tes Eng-lein her-

nie-der zu der Welt. Die hü-ten sei-nen Schlum-mer ge-treu die gan-ze

Nacht, schlaf süß und sanft, klein Haa-kon, auch dei-ne Mut-ter wacht.

III.

I Love Thee
(Ich liebe dich; Jeg elsker dig)

Er - den, ich lie - be dich, ich lie - be dich, ich lie - be dich in Zeit und

E - wig-keit! Ich lie - be dich in Zeit und E - wig-keit!

Ich den - ke dein, kann stets nur dei - ner

den - - ken, nur dei - nem

Glück ist die - - ses Herz ge-weiht;

lie - - be dich in Zeit und E - - wig-keit!

IV.

She Is So White
(Wenn einst . . ./Sie ist so weiss; Hun er saa hvid)

Wenn einst sie lag an mei-ner Brust, ver-meint ich wohl in

höch-ster Lust, ich lieb-te jetzt sie schon so sehr, daß ich sie nie könnt lie—ben

mehr!

Da nun sie nahm der Tod ans Herz, er-

fahr ich's, ach, im tief-sten Schmerz: Wie ich sie auch ge-liebt vor-her, ich lieb sie jetzt doch

noch   viel mehr!

V.
The Princess
(Die Prinzessin; Prinsessen)

VI.

To Springtime
(An den Lenz; Jeg giver mig digt til våren)

Allegro vivace

Lenz soll mein Lied er - klin - gen, es soll ihn zu-rück uns brin-gen.Wie säu-met er nur so

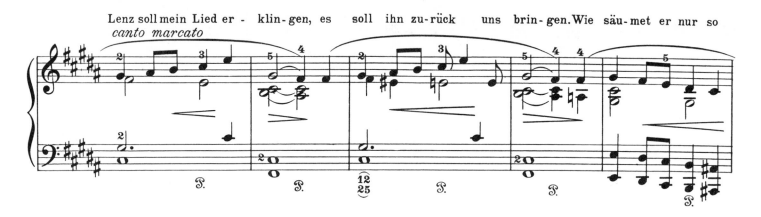

lang und macht unsern Her - zen bang, er - tö - ne ihm denn mein Sang!

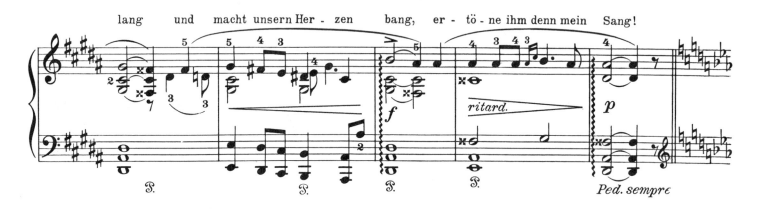

Schon zwit - schern die Vög - - lein

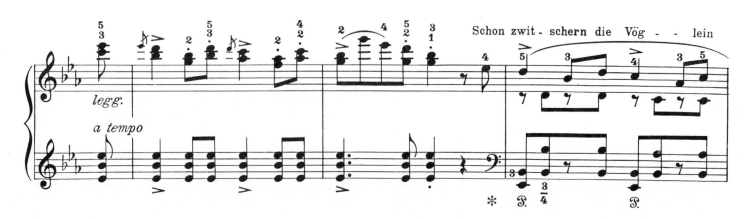

Peer Gynt Suite No. 1, Op. 46
I.
Morning Mood
(Morgenstimmung; Morgenstemning)

II.
Åse's Death
(Åses Tod; Åses död)

III.
Anitra's Dance
(Anitras Tanz; Anitras dans)

Tempo di Mazurka   ♩ = 160

★) The trills without concluding notes.

IV.
In the Hall of the Mountain King
(In der Halle des Bergkönigs; I dovregubbens hal)

Piano Pieces after His Own Songs (II), Op. 52
Klavierstücke nach eigenen Liedern
I.
A Mother's Grief
(Mutterschmerz; Modersorg)

O wie hell mein Le - ben war, blickte noch mein Knäb - lein drein.

Dun - kel ward's für im - mer-dar, da er - losch sein Au - gen - schein.

ach, wie schwer um

cresc.

Ach, wie leer, wie öd und leer ohn' ihn nun Haus und Her - ze_

ihn, wie schwer die Brust von Gram und Schmer - - - ze!

a tempo

fz poco rit.

p

poco rit.

a tempo

pp

War - um nahmst, o Herr - gott mein, dein Ge - schenk so schnell du zu - rück!

cantabile
mf

pp

II.
The First Meeting
(Erstes Begegnen; Det første møde)

III.

The Poet's Heart
(Des Dichters Herz)

Allegro molto ed agitato

IV.
Solvejg's Song
(Solvejgs Lied; Solvejgs sang)

du mir nah, und har-rest du dort o - ben, so tref-fen wir uns da, so tref - fen wir uns

Ah...

da!

Allegretto con moto

Tempo I

V.
Love
(Liebe; Kjaerlighed)

VI.
The Old Mother
(Die alte Mutter; Gamle mor)

hauch - test in die Brust hin - ein ihm Lie - des Sang und

Two Melodies, Op. 53
Zwei Melodien
I.

Norwegian
(Norwegisch)

Repetizione Dal Segno 𝄋 sin' al Fine

II.

The First Meeting
(Erstes Begegnen; Det første møde)

Peer Gynt Suite No. 2, Op. 55
I.
Ingrid's Lament
(Ingrids Klage; Ingrids klage)

II.
Arabian Dance
(Arabischer Tanz; Arabisk dans)

III.
Peer Gynt's Return Home
(Peer Gynts Heimkehr; Peer Gynts hjemfart)

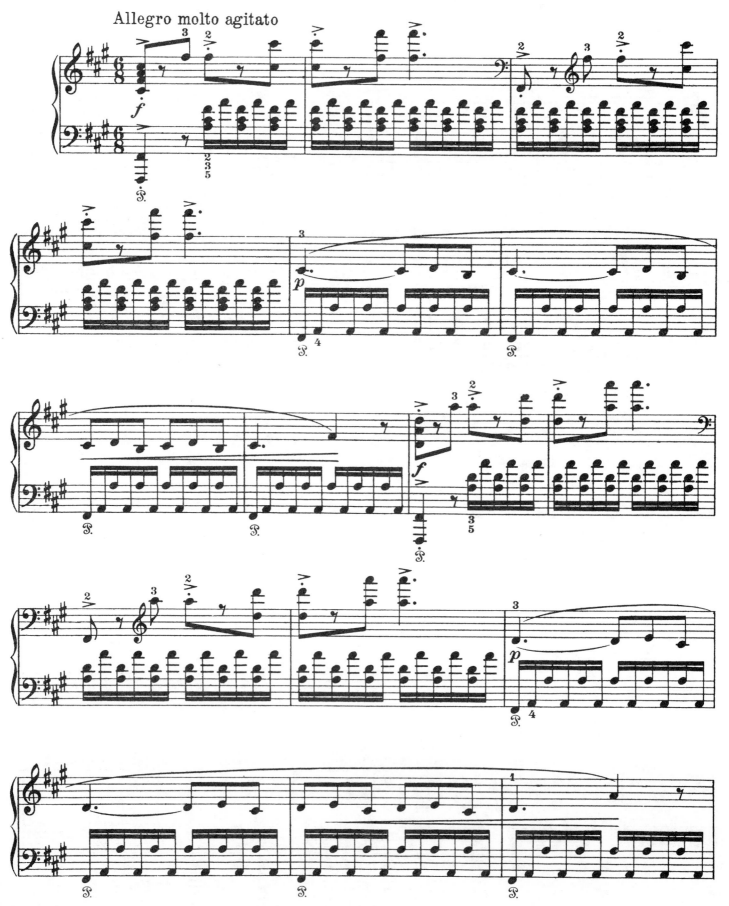

attacca

IV.
Solvejg's Song
(Solvejgs Lied; Solvejgs sang)

Der Win - ter mag schei-den, der Frühling vergehn, der Früh - ling ver - gehn,

der Sommer mag ver - wel - ken, das Jahr ver - wehn, das Jahr ver - wehn;

du kehrest mir zu - rü - cke, ge - wiß, du wirst mein, ge - wiß, du wirst mein, ich

hab es ver - spro - chen, ich harre treu-lich dein, ich har - re treu - lich dein. Ah...

Moods, Op. 73
Stimmungen
I.
Resignation

II.
Scherzo-Impromptu

Allegro capriccioso M.M. ♩ = 120

III.
Night Ride
(Natligt ridt)

*) The melody is to be played by the thumb throughout the passage.

IV.
Folksong
(Folketone)

V.
Study (Hommage à Chopin)
(Studie [Hommage à Chopin])

VI.
Students' Serenade
(Studenternes serenade)

VII.
The Mountaineer's Song
(Lualåt)

Nordraak's Funeral March, WoOp.
Sörgemarsch over Rikard Nordraak

Three Piano Pieces, WoOp.
Drei Klavierstücke
I.

White Clouds*
(Hvide skyer)

*) Only sketches were on hand for this piece, which was completed by Julius Röntgen.

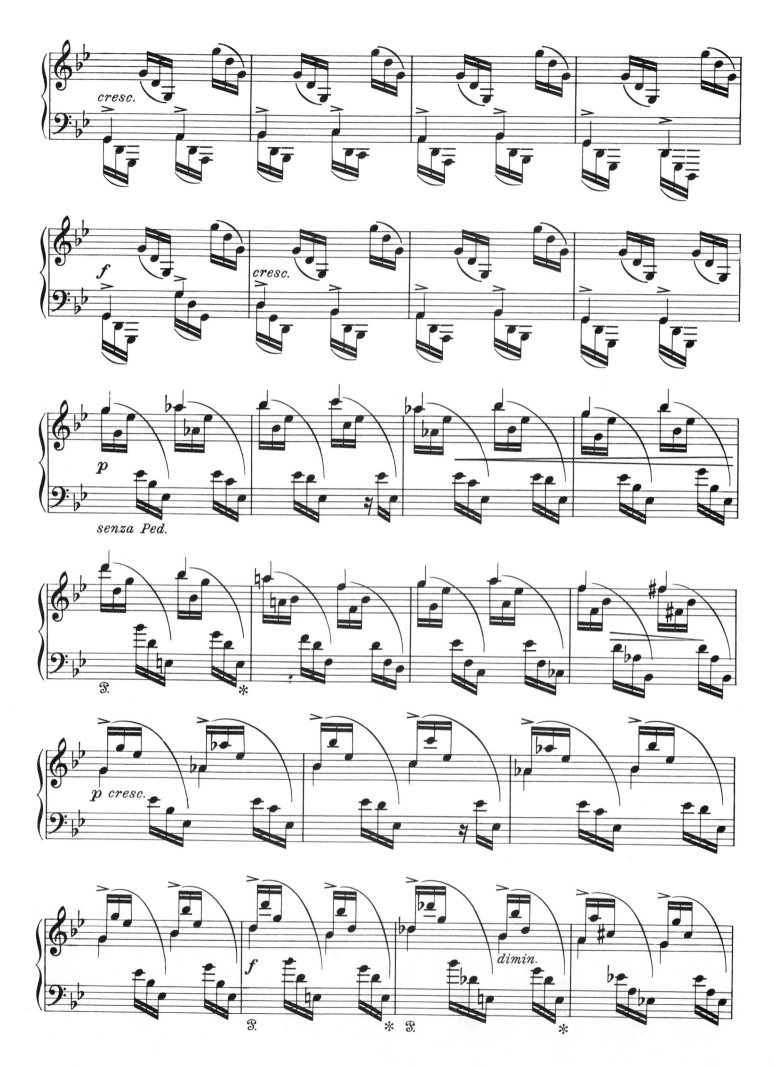

II.
Gnomes' Tune
(Tusselslåt)

III.
The Dance Goes On
(Dansen går)

THE END

Dover Piano and Keyboard Editions

THE WELL-TEMPERED CLAVIER: Books I and II, Complete, Johann Sebastian Bach. All 48 preludes and fugues in all major and minor keys. Authoritative Bach-Gesellschaft edition. Explanation of ornaments in English, tempo indications, music corrections. 208pp. 9⅜ × 12¼. 24532-2 Pa. **$9.95**

KEYBOARD MUSIC, J. S. Bach. Bach-Gesellschaft edition. For harpsichord, piano, other keyboard instruments. English Suites, French Suites, Six Partitas, Goldberg Variations, Two-Part Inventions, Three-Part Sinfonias. 312pp. 8⅛ × 11. 22360-4 Pa. **$11.95**

ITALIAN CONCERTO, CHROMATIC FANTASIA AND FUGUE AND OTHER WORKS FOR KEYBOARD, Johann Sebastian Bach. Sixteen of Bach's best-known, most-performed and most-recorded works for the keyboard, reproduced from the authoritative Bach-Gesellschaft edition. 112pp. 9 × 12. 25387-2 Pa. **$8.95**

COMPLETE KEYBOARD TRANSCRIPTIONS OF CONCERTOS BY BAROQUE COMPOSERS, Johann Sebastian Bach. Sixteen concertos by Vivaldi, Telemann and others, transcribed for solo keyboard instruments. Bach-Gesellschaft edition. 128pp. 9⅜ × 12¼. 25529-8 Pa. **$8.95**

ORGAN MUSIC, J. S. Bach. Bach-Gesellschaft edition. 93 works. 6 Trio Sonatas, German Organ Mass, Orgelbüchlein, Six Schubler Chorales, 18 Choral Preludes. 357pp. 8⅛ × 11. 22359-0 Pa. **$12.95**

COMPLETE PRELUDES AND FUGUES FOR ORGAN, Johann Sebastian Bach. All 25 of Bach's complete sets of preludes and fugues (i.e. compositions written as pairs), from the authoritative Bach-Gesellschaft edition. 168pp. 8⅜ × 11. 24816-X Pa. **$9.95**

TOCCATAS, FANTASIAS, PASSACAGLIA AND OTHER WORKS FOR ORGAN, J. S. Bach. Over 20 best-loved works including Toccata and Fugue in D minor, BWV 565; Passacaglia and Fugue in C minor, BWV 582, many more. Bach-Gesellschaft edition. 176pp. 9 × 12. 25403-8 Pa. **$9.95**

TWO- AND THREE-PART INVENTIONS, J. S. Bach. Reproduction of original autograph ms. Edited by Eric Simon. 62pp. 8⅛ × 11. 21982-8 Pa. **$8.95**

THE 36 FANTASIAS FOR KEYBOARD, Georg Philipp Telemann. Graceful compositions by 18th-century master. 1923 Breslauer edition. 80pp. 8⅛ × 11. 25365-1 Pa. **$5.95**

GREAT KEYBOARD SONATAS, Carl Philipp Emanuel Bach. Comprehensive two-volume edition contains 51 sonatas by second, most important son of Johann Sebastian Bach. Originality, rich harmony, delicate workmanship. Authoritative French edition. Total of 384pp. 8⅜ × 11¼. Series I 24853-4 Pa. **$9.95**
Series II 24854-2 Pa. **$10.95**

KEYBOARD WORKS/Series One: Ordres I-XIII; Series Two: Ordres XIV-XXVII and Miscellaneous Pieces, François Couperin. Over 200 pieces. Reproduced directly from edition prepared by Johannes Brahms and Friedrich Chrysander. Total of 496pp. 8⅛ × 11.
Series I 25795-9 Pa. **$10.95**
Series II 25796-7 Pa. **$11.95**

KEYBOARD WORKS FOR SOLO INSTRUMENTS, G. F. Handel. 35 neglected works from Handel's vast oeuvre, originally jotted down as improvisations. Includes Eight Great Suites, others. New sequence. 174pp. 9⅜ × 12¼. 24338-9 Pa. **$9.95**

WORKS FOR ORGAN AND KEYBOARD, Jan Pieterszoon Sweelinck. Nearly all of early Dutch composer's difficult-to-find keyboard works. Chorale variations; toccatas, fantasias; variations on secular, dance tunes. Also, incomplete and/or modified works, plus fantasia by John Bull. 272pp. 9 × 12. 24935-2 Pa. **$12.95**

ORGAN WORKS, Dietrich Buxtehude. Complete organ works of extremely influential pre-Bach composer. Toccatas, preludes, chorales, more. Definitive Breitkopf & Härtel edition. 320pp. 8⅜ × 11¼. (Available in U.S. only) 25682-0 Pa. **$12.95**

THE FUGUES ON THE MAGNIFICAT FOR ORGAN OR KEYBOARD, Johann Pachelbel. 94 pieces representative of Pachelbel's magnificent contribution to keyboard composition; can be played on the organ, harpsichord or piano. 100pp. 9 × 12. (Available in U.S. only) 25037-7 Pa. **$7.95**

MY LADY NEVELLS BOOKE OF VIRGINAL MUSIC, William Byrd. 42 compositions in modern notation from 1591 ms. For any keyboard instrument. 245pp. 8⅛ × 11. 22246-2 Pa. **$13.95**

ELIZABETH ROGERS HIR VIRGINALL BOOKE, edited with calligraphy by Charles J. F. Cofone. All 112 pieces from noted 1656 manuscript, most never before published. Composers include Thomas Brewer, William Byrd, Orlando Gibbons, etc. 125pp. 9 × 12. 23138-0 Pa. **$10.95**

THE FITZWILLIAM VIRGINAL BOOK, edited by J. Fuller Maitland, W. B. Squire. Famous early 17th-century collection of keyboard music, 300 works by Morley, Byrd, Bull, Gibbons, etc. Modern notation. Total of 938pp. 8⅜ × 11. Two-vol. set. 21068-5, 21069-3 Pa. **$33.90**

GREAT KEYBOARD SONATAS, Series I and Series II, Domenico Scarlatti. 78 of the most popular sonatas reproduced from the G. Ricordi edition edited by Alessandro Longo. Total of 320pp. 8⅜ × 11¼.
Series I 24996-4 Pa. **$8.95**
Series II 25003-2 Pa. **$8.95**

SONATAS AND FANTASIES FOR THE PIANO, W. A. Mozart, edited by Nathan Broder. Finest, most accurate edition, based on autographs and earliest editions. 19 sonatas, plus Fantasy and Fugue in C, K.394, Fantasy in C Minor, K.396, Fantasy in D Minor, K.397. 352pp. 9 × 12. (Available in U.S. only) 25417-8 Pa. **$16.50**

COMPLETE PIANO SONATAS, Joseph Haydn. 52 sonatas reprinted from authoritative Breitkopf & Härtel edition. Extremely clear and readable; ample space for notes, analysis. 464pp. 9⅜ × 12¼.
24726-0 Pa. **$10.95**
24727-9 Pa. **$11.95**

BAGATELLES, RONDOS AND OTHER SHORTER WORKS FOR PIANO, Ludwig van Beethoven. Most popular and most performed shorter works, including Rondo a capriccio in G and Andante in F. Breitkopf & Härtel edition. 128pp. 9⅜ × 12¼. 25392-9 Pa. **$8.95**

COMPLETE VARIATIONS FOR SOLO PIANO, Ludwig van Beethoven. Contains all 21 sets of Beethoven's piano variations, including the extremely popular *Diabelli Variations, Op. 120*. 240pp. 9⅜ × 12¼. 25188-8 Pa. **$11.95**

COMPLETE PIANO SONATAS, Ludwig van Beethoven. All sonatas in fine Schenker edition, with fingering, analytical material. One of best modern editions. 615pp. 9 × 12. Two-vol. set. 23134-8, 23135-6 Pa. **$25.90**

COMPLETE SONATAS FOR PIANOFORTE SOLO, Franz Schubert. All 15 sonatas. Breitkopf and Härtel edition. 293pp. 9⅜ × 12¼. 22647-6 Pa. **$13.95**

DANCES FOR SOLO PIANO, Franz Schubert. Over 350 waltzes, minuets, landler, ecossaises, other charming, melodic dance compositions reprinted from the authoritative Breitkopf & Härtel edition. 192pp. 9⅜ × 12¼. 26107-7 Pa. **$10.95**

Available from your music dealer or write for ***free*** *Music Catalog to*
Dover Publications, Inc., Dept. MUBI, 31 East 2nd Street, Mineola, N.Y. 11501.